PROUT
EXPLAINED

PROUT EXPLAINED

A BRIEF INTRODUCTION TO THE PROGRESSIVE UTILIZATION THEORY

DADA VEDAPRAJINANANDA

Innerworld Publications
San Germán, Puerto Rico
www.innerworldpublications.com

Library of Congress Catalog Card Number: 2020951275

Cover Design © Donald Acosta and Kevin Farge

The front cover image is a symbolic depiction of the social cycle, the cyclical change of leadership in society, a concept introduced by P.R. Sarkar and explained in this book.

ISBN 978-1-881717-81-2

Introduction

HUMANITY STANDS AT THE brink of a critical juncture. Immense disparities of wealth, unending war, global pandemics, climate change, and the threat of total economic collapse have created a crisis unprecedented in our recent history.

To overcome these crises, we will have to use intelligence, wisdom and love. However, our dilemma is that the present economic system - capitalism - and its related political structures, place the life and death decision-making regarding these problems in the hands of people who are primarily seeking to enrich themselves or their backers. Intelligence, love and wisdom have little or no role to play in their deliberations.

Is there a way out? Is there an alternative to capitalism? Can we get the human household in order and create a world where all people (and not just a few) live with dignity, have their basic needs fulfilled and are free to reach their highest potential? The adherents of Karl Marx's theories tried to create an alternative to capitalism in the 20th century but their efforts were, in most respects, extremely unsuccessful.

At the height of the Cold War, when the clash of communism and capitalism was intense and problematic for humanity, an Indian philosopher, P.R. Sarkar, put forward an alternative social and economic theory which he called the Progressive Utilization Theory (known by its acronym Prout). Sarkar claimed that the application of this theory could bring prosperity and social justice to the world, overcoming the problems of both capitalism and communism.

Today, capitalism has been shaken by a global pandemic and economic instability comparable to the Great Depression of the 1930s. It is in this context that Prout takes on a new importance. In the following pages I want to show how this economic and social model can help humanity surmount the current crisis and build the foundations of a world in which all people can flourish in harmony with the planet and all its living beings.

The Universal
Commons

O NE OF THE CAUSES of our present predic-
ament is a narrow approach to the world,
in which individuals, groups and nation-states
struggle to gain exclusive ownership, control and
use of finite resources. A better way to look at
the world is to understand that we are part of a
Universal Commons and are here to utilize things
to our best capacity.

The concept of a Universal Commons is not
unique to Prout. "In European political texts, the
common wealth was the totality of the material
riches of the world, such as the air, the water, the
soil and the seed, all nature's bounty regarded as
the inheritance of humanity as a whole, to be
shared together."[1] Sarkar calls this commonwealth
our cosmic inheritance.

From this standpoint, we are the stewards of
wealth, not the ultimate owners. We should use
things as if we are in a joint family. If children live

in a family with their parents, they don't claim different parts of the house as exclusively being theirs. Also, if we are living together as a family it would be unacceptable for any one person to hoard the entire food pantry. Prout says that humans must live together as a family and harmoniously share the wealth of the world.

How shall we do this? Let's look at the economy and our system of government and see how Prout could accomplish it.

The Three-Tiered Economy and Economic Democracy

A LMOST ALL THE COUNTRIES of the world are nominal democracies with regularly scheduled elections but in all cases, these are political democracies, not economic democracies. People have the right to vote for political leaders, but they have no little or no rights in the economic sphere. In economic democracy people will have a say in decisions that affect their economic livelihood. Democracy will be extended to the workplace and the economy will be decentralized. "In economic democracy local people will have the power to make all economic decisions (and) to produce commodities on the basis of collective necessity."[2]

In addition, the intent of Prout is to bring about a society in which there is maximum development of human and natural resources leading to the well-being of all. One way to move towards the goals of economic democracy and the best utilization of resources would be to organize our economic enterprises in three tiers.

1. The Private Sector

This tier or sector of the economy would include small businesses and enterprises that employ few people and do not deal with essential needs. Small restaurants, repair shops, custom fabrication, lawyers, accountants, and other similar activities are examples of enterprises in this sector. These businesses are most efficiently run privately by individuals, partnerships or families. This sector is where private enterprise would thrive and not harm the larger society.

2. The Cooperative Sector

When enterprises grow larger, employing more people and dealing with the necessities of life such as food, shelter, clothing, education and medicine, then individual ownership and management becomes problematic because after a certain size the success of a firm is no longer clearly dependent on the owner. At that point, a good arrangement for medium-sized businesses is the cooperative. In addition, exclusive private ownership of enterprises producing vital necessities can result in outcomes that are not beneficial to society.

All the workers in a cooperative are shareholders and they elect a managing board. Each worker has some say in determining the direction of the co-op, but the managing board handles operational decisions. A large portion of an economy could be run by cooperatives and this would help establish economic democracy.

It is not uncommon that industrial firms are bought by foreign owners, and when these owners decide that one of their foreign holdings is unprofitable, they can simply decide to a shut a factory. The workers of that factory have no say in this decision made by a small board of directors based in a foreign country. Those workers have the right to vote in political elections in their country and thus could be said to enjoy political democracy, but they would have to sit silently on the sidelines while decisions about their economic livelihood were being made undemocratically by a few people in another country.

Worker-owned cooperatives substitute this form of absentee ownership with local ownership - building enterprises that are directly tied to the needs of the people working there and the surrounding community. In addition, the strife of labor vs. management centering around issues of worker exploitation are avoided in this model.

Worker-owned businesses exist all over the

world. In the U.S. there are close to 400 worker-owned cooperatives with a total yearly turnover exceeding $400 million[3] and in the Basque region of Northern Spain the Mondragon Corporation, a federation of worker-owned cooperatives, employs more than 70,000 workers and has a yearly turnover in excess of 12 billion Euros.

Building up a cooperative sector, in the midst of a capitalist system, will be one of the biggest challenges in implementing the three-tiered economic model. Already existing large-scale capitalist enterprises enjoy advantages of scale and can offer their goods at lower prices, for example. That is why Sarkar suggests that the government should provide "protective armor" in the form of "exemption from sales tax, duties, etc. This protection should be withdrawn slowly. Protective armor should be limited to essential commodities only."[4] This sort of help would enable cooperatives to get a toehold and eventually thrive.

3. The Public Sector (Key Industries)

There are economic activities which run on a larger scale and with wide-ranging impacts on the greater economy. Transportation, communication, mineral extraction and communications are some of the large-scale enterprises which require a form of ownership and management that is neither private nor cooperative. Sarkar has called these key industries. We could also call this the public sector because this is the area of activity that affects everyone and in which we all have a common interest. According to Prout, these enterprises should be managed by the local state government. If there is no strong local government (as might arise in unitary political systems, where there are no state or provincial governments) a public board could be set up in that geographic area to run the project.

Sarkar emphasizes that in cases where governmental bodies manage the key industries these bodies should be immediate, local government and not central governments.

Some people are alarmed by talk of public management and government management of key industries and utilities. They attribute corruption, bureaucracy and inefficiency and other woes to the government. In some circles, "the government" is the bogey man responsible for innumerable problems.

Without getting into the "good" and the "bad" of government, let's look at it another way. If we would not be comfortable with some sort of public ownership and management of key sectors of the economy, are we happy to let unseen and unnamed shareholders and private corporate interests run these industries for the sake of their own profit?

Will we have more "freedom" if private companies run the activities of the public sector? In a Proutist system, if a public utility doesn't do the job properly then it would be subject to oversight and correction by the locally elected government. If the government administration is not regulating or managing things properly, then it could be replaced in the next election. But who can correct the wrongs committed by private interests working in the public sector?

There is another thing to consider about key industries. Decisions about mineral extraction, particularly when it comes to the fossil fuel industry, will affect the whole society today and perhaps for generations to come. Should those decisions be made by a corporate board acting to maximize profit, or by elected representatives making their decisions based on the public good? A privately-owned company will make decisions based on immediate economic gains, but usually will ignore pollution, climate change and other consequences to society that lie outside their yearly profit and loss balance sheet.

Decentralized Balanced Economies and Regional Self-Sufficiency

I N ADDITION TO REORGANIZING the economy according to the three tiers of private, cooperative and public sectors, there are also other economic problems that we need to address with a new outlook. Great disparities in economic development exist between regions and localities even within one country and certainly among the many countries and regions of the world.

Within a country economic activity is often centralized around manufacturing centers, while other areas, usually rural, remain underdeveloped and less prosperous. With fewer job opportunities in the rural areas, young people flee to the cities. The underdeveloped areas are not only economically disadvantaged but suffer from less activity and development in the arts, culture and education.

Under capitalism economic centralization is encouraged because the task of maximizing profit is the main goal. However, if the goal of our economic activity is to produce goods for consumption and the satisfaction of the public, then economic decentralization makes a lot of sense. Decentralization will make it possible for different regions to produce the goods and services that they need and to guarantee the minimum requirements of life to those living in the region. Most importantly, decentralization will prevent the regional disparity that causes economic hardship in some regions while others bask in prosperity.

Sarkar describes it as follows:

> *"In the decentralized economy of PROUT.... production is for consumption, and the minimum requirements of life will be guaranteed to all. All regions will get ample scope to develop their economic potentiality, so the problems of a floating population or overcrowding in urban centers will not be allowed to arise."* [5]

The current centralized capitalist economy leads to all kinds of social and economic problems. Young people deprived of economic opportunities become alienated, crime spikes in overcrowded urban areas and people are forced to leave their native areas in search of jobs elsewhere.

The best way to reverse this situation is to place some industries and supporting services in rural areas. In this way, excessive congestion of urban areas will be avoided, and strong regional centers will provide employment and services to previously neglected rural areas. On the international level, the task of implementing decentralized and balanced economic development is of prime importance.

How could we bring about the kind of balance in which people will not be compelled to leave their native lands and make dangerous journeys in search of a better life elsewhere? The simple answer is that we have to make sure there is no need for anyone to leave because there are economic opportunities right at their doorsteps.

Why are there no opportunities in lesser developed nations? Some people believe that the people in these countries do not work hard, are immoral, not intelligent and even criminal. Is this viewpoint correct?

The present world has developed very unevenly. The commercial and industrial revolutions began in Europe in the 1600s and 1800s respectively. Europe and the US developed their industries and commerce rapidly and colonized large parts of Africa, Asia and South America. In the 1960s the colonized areas achieved *political* independence. I put emphasis on the word political, because in most cases the former colonies did not achieve economic independence. Multinational corporations (based in developed countries) owned the valuable mineral extraction enterprises and other industries of these newly independent countries. Profits of these foreign-held assets were sent abroad and not used in the development of the newly independent countries. If you do even superficial research you will see that the history of colonization and continued foreign ownership of vital economic assets is a contributing factor to the current imbalance of developed and developing nations in today's world.

Under capitalism it makes economic sense to concentrate manufacturing in one area because suppliers are close by and there is a good supply of labor and infrastructure. This works in the short run, but the result is often a countryside that is impoverished while urban areas becomes islands of prosperity. An extension of this problem is seen when entire nations depend primarily on agriculture or basic mineral extraction and ship their products abroad without finishing them or adding value to them. These countries are less prosperous than the ones which have manufacturing and more diverse economics. A country that exports raw cocoa may have to purchase the chocolate bars that are made in another country!

So, what is the solution? Instead of creating "Banana Republics" it would be far better if currently lesser-developed nations could build diverse economies with manufacturing, services, etc., alongside their raw material and agricultural production. Instead of exporting raw materials, these countries would finish the products and add value to them before exporting them.

Prout's founder, P.R. Sarkar, said that a country with a balanced economy should employ a portion of its population in agriculture, another portion in the sector that provides equipment for agriculture, and another portion in a sector that finished, or added value, to the raw agricultural produce. The rest of the population could be employed in manufacturing and services. A country, or a group of countries in a geographic region, with a diverse and balanced economy would become prosperous and provide economic opportunities to local people, who wouldn't have to flee to other countries.

In addition, the encouragement of balanced economic planning and implementation could help developed countries as well. Due to current trade policies the US no longer manufactures many goods, and not only has this brought unemployment and blight to previously thriving industrial areas, the country finds itself in a difficult position when global supply chains are disrupted by unforeseen developments (like pandemics or war).

It is not easy to change centuries of economic activity but there are other factors that are within human control. Underdeveloped areas that want to build an industrial sector often go through a difficult initial phase. When I was growing up, I remember people joking about some product that would have "made in Japan" stamped on it. "Made in Japan" meant it was a cheap imitation of low quality. Today no one laughs at "made in Japan" because Japan was able to successfully transition and become a high-end manufacturing economy. Presently underdeveloped countries can make this transition, if they are "allowed" to make it.

Present trade policies do not favor the diversification of economies in lesser developed areas. The slogans of "free trade" and "globalization" are in vogue now. This means that, according to supporters of free trade, tariffs should come down and everyone should be allowed to sell their products anywhere without restriction. Countries that are developing a new manufacturing sector will at first produce wobbly products, like the "made in Japan" items of the early 1950s. If they are not allowed to protect these products from foreign competition, then the nascent manufacturing sectors will never become successful. Instead of free trade, developing areas need fair trade, and they should be allowed to protect the areas of their economy that will eventually bring them to full prosperity. The demonstrations at the World Trade Organization meetings in Seattle in 2000, and at subsequent rounds of negotiations revolved around the trade tensions between developing and developed economies.

In a more just world, developing nations and regions would be allowed to build up their new industries and move towards more diverse economies. If one country did not have enough resources or a topography suited towards building a self-sufficient unit, it could join with other nearby countries to form a self-sufficient economic zone. Sarkar envisioned the creation of self-sufficient economic zones based on common economic, linguistic, cultural and geographical features to create prosperity in all parts of the world. As the different economic zones of the world reach parity, it might be possible, one day, to envision a world that is one economic zone (such as we have today in the US) but until that day comes, we should do whatever is possible to encourage the development of self-sufficient economic zones around the world.

. *"When the entire wealth of the universe is the common patrimony of all living beings, can the system in which some roll in luxury, while others, deprived of a morsel of food, shrivel up and starve to death bit by bit, be said to be just?"* [6]

The Fundamental Principles for Creating a Just Society

THOSE WHO SUPPORT THE present capitalist economic and social system argue that it is very efficient and powerful because individuals are free to produce and accumulate wealth. Adam Smith spoke of the "invisible hand" of private self-interest which, he claimed, ultimately ends up bringing about the greater good of society.

Incentives for individuals to work and strive are indeed beneficial for society. If everyone were to get equal pay whether they worked or didn't work, then there would be stagnation. During the 1980s I used to visit Poland which was then a communist country. One afternoon I was walking with a friend past a road where a work crew was supposed to be fixing the highway. It was in the afternoon and the work crew was just sitting there. I asked my friend what was going on and he said, "They know that whether they work or don't work they are going to get paid, so they are just relaxing as much as they can."

Individual action and selfish motivation however are not the only engines of human progress. In the early stages of human evolution, our species was not the strongest one in a physical sense. Giant mammals with sharp teeth roamed the plains but the physically weaker humans had more mental strength and were able to work in unison to trap and kill the larger animals. Had each human been living alone and struggling alone they could not have prevailed.

Harnessing the power of cooperation, coupled with incentives for individuals to work would provide an ideal framework for economic and social progress. But how to do it? Capitalism has unleashed individualism and tremendous wealth has been accumulated, but the distribution of that wealth is completely distorted in favor of a few. On the other hand, countries following Marxism placed emphasis on the state at the expense of individuals.

Prout proposes an alternative way, a path that would enable both individuals and society to flourish. This approach is based on five fundamental principles.

1. No Individual should be allowed to accumulate wealth without the clear permission and approval of society.

This principle hits at the fundamental defect of our current society. Currently, individuals or families can amass wealth even if it results in the starvation of millions. In addition, wealthy people can amass wealth to such a degree that they are able to "buy" control of the government. There is no check on wealth accumulation and up until recently there has hardly been any public discussion of the matter.

There is some public discourse about a social safety net and a minimum wage for those at the bottom of the economic ladder. Or to put it another way, some people would like to see a floor in the economic house so that people will not be deprived of basic needs. But there is less discussion about a ceiling on the economic house. The idea that society should have some say over how much individuals accumulate is rarely, if ever, proposed. And when someone does question the right of the wealthiest to keep accumulating, there is a howl of opposition.

The counter-argument is that caps on wealth would stifle incentive and innovation and economic activity would come to a halt. The very rich people are the job creators and wealth creators, goes this argument, and their wealth will eventually trickle down to the rest of the society. This is not just an academic argument; it is actual policy in the U.S. Instead of capping wealth and income (through taxation) we are currently offering tax cuts to the wealthy in hopes that this will encourage them to "create more wealth, create more jobs."

This is called supply-side economics or trickle-down economics. But how is it working out? The richest families in the U.S. have as much wealth as the bottom 40% of the entire country. The trickle-down process is not very efficient in providing for the well-being of many but very good at enriching the few. A cap on wealth accumulation could stop trickle-down economics in its tracks and pave the way for a more just distribution of wealth as well as curbing the distortion of investment into inappropriate and wasteful speculation.

2. There should be maximum utilization and rational distribution of the mundane, supramundane and spiritual potentialities of the universe.

We are currently doing a good job of churning up the earth and manufacturing products to satisfy the needs of some people, but we are not so good at distributing the products and meeting the needs of all people. In the first principle, the concept of a wealth cap was introduced and whenever this kind of discussion is started, the proponents of capitalism say, "How will people be motivated to create and produce if they are not allowed to accumulate as much as they can?" It is a valid question. Without some incentive or motivation society would stagnate. The concept of "from each according to his/her ability, to each according to his/her need" sounds good (to some ears at least) but has never really worked in practice. One reason that it has never worked is that leaders of nominally socialist or communist societies often did not lead frugal lives and the large disparities between the masses and the leaders created resentment and lethargy.

Prout's second principle calls for maximum utilization and rational distribution. What would rational distribution look like? Everyone in our society should be able to have the purchasing capacity enabling them to acquire the minimum necessities of life. Just as we want a ceiling in our economic household, we need a floor and must see to it that no one falls through this floor and is left destitute. But even if all people were able to procure their minimum necessities how would we motivate the innovative, creative, and imaginative people of our society to do more and use their talents to improve themselves and humanity?

Rational distribution means that once the minimum necessities are assured for all people, then the extra portion should be given to meritorious people to encourage them to do even better work. Today we have the concept of giving large bonuses to corporate CEOs, but this is not what Prout means by rational distribution. The bonuses and salaries given to CEOs create a huge gap which demoralizes most workers and doesn't encourage them to do better work. In 1980 the ratio of CEO salaries and median worker was 40 to 1. In 2016 it was 347 to 1 according to the Institute for Policy Studies as reported in the *LA Times*.[7]

The Proutist conception of rational distribution is to have a much narrower gap. Ravi Batra, an economist who has long been a proponent of Prout, proposed 10:1 as a good ratio between the highest and lowest wages. In the Mondragon Corporation of Spain - the world's largest worker-owned cooperative - the ratio is presently 9 to 1. Whatever the number society finally decides upon, the idea is that all workers should get a wage that will allow them to purchase the minimum necessities of life and that individuals who make exceptional contributions to economic and social well-being will be awarded with greater amenities and comforts so that they can continue to innovate. As productivity and overall wealth grows, minimum wages and amenities will rise and the rewards to meritorious people will also rise. Today, we have the exact opposite happening. As the economy grows, the gap between the median and highest salaries increases. This is not particularly fair, nor is it rational. It is not rational because the excessive rewards given to those at the top usually far exceeds the value of the contributions that these bonus-earners have produced.

The second principle of Prout also calls for the maximum utilization of mundane, supra mundane and spiritual potentialities of the universe. "Mundane" clearly refers to the physical resources of the world and forests, rivers, minerals, etc., are what we commonly think about when we consider using or developing natural resources. We should use the physical resources around us to satisfy genuine human needs.

Supramundane and spiritual potentialities are not so clear. When considering supramundane and spiritual potentials of resources we must look beyond their outward physical value and consider how they help humanity in deeper ways.

Here is one way to look at it. Consider a forest. If you add up the economic value of all the trees of a forest you will come to some total. But, is the number which aggregates the physical worth of the forest the only indicator of the forest's value to humanity? What about the sheer beauty and pleasure that a forest provides to people who use it for recreation? The aesthetic appreciation and inspiration of the forest is its supramundane potential and it would be foolish to cut all the trees and think that there has been maximum utilization of the forest.

Going further with this idea, suppose there is an ancient church or temple where people have carried out their spiritual practices for many years or even millennia, or a cemetery and worship plot used by indigenous people. What is the value of that piece of property? Can you measure the square feet or meters and then compare it to other real estate in the area? Should we convert that building into a bowling alley or dance hall? No, the accrued spiritual value of the building or land would greatly outweigh the possible physical market value, and maximum utilization would mean that it would be preserved for its original purpose or something similar.

Utilizing and distributing resources to individuals in a rational way is important, but there are some other factors that need to be considered. For example, during the Cold War, the Soviet Union launched satellites and sent people into space, and these scientific feats were celebrated in the state-run media. The Soviet citizens were made to feel proud of these accomplishments; however, their standard of living lagged behind people living in capitalist countries. Clearly, the needs of the state were prioritized over the production of consumer goods. However, on the other side of the Iron Curtain things were not (and are still not) perfect. Some individuals grew wealthy while social infrastructure often crumbled.

How to get the balance right? Why not try to promote the well-being of individuals and, at the same time, meet the needs of the society? The third principle of Prout addresses this issue. It says:

3. There should be maximum utilization of the physical, metaphysical and spiritual potentialities of the unit and collective bodies of human society.

The good of society depends on the well-being of its members and the well-being of individuals also depends on the health of the overall society. The two go hand in hand. The needs of individuals for food, clothing, shelter, education and medical care must be met if a society is to thrive. It is a folly to boast of national accomplishment by pointing to a few costly military projects while the general population is living at a subsistence level. It is also a folly to consider a country developed by pointing to the inventions of a few gifted people, while the rest of society is uneducated or undereducated.

Individuals should be able to meet their basic needs and to thrive, to develop themselves physically, mentally and spiritually. The scientific or artistic success of a few people can't make up for masses of people who are uneducated or undereducated and that is why a healthy society would enable everyone, and not just elites, to avail themselves of all opportunities to develop. It is a tremendous loss if large segments of the human family are deprived of education and other avenues of personal growth.

However, personal growth doesn't mean the exclusive cultivation of selfishness. If individuals do not have an appreciation that their well-being also depends on the overall health of their society, and if they do not develop a sense of responsibility towards their community, then it will be difficult to establish the greater good.

Many of the institutions, such as cooperatives, that we are proposing as the solution to the problems of today depend on encouraging and enhancing human qualities like cooperation, social service and love for humanity. If people are devoid of these traits, then the greed and selfishness that have plagued modern-day capitalism will haunt and ultimately destroy all efforts to build a healthier society.

P.R. Sarkar said, "The absence of spiritual morality will break the backbone of the collectivity. So, for the sake of collective welfare one will have to awaken spirituality in individuals."[8] He goes on to explain that each human being has the potential for infinite physical, mental and spiritual development, and that we must do everything possible to bring this potential to fruition.

Getting all elements in place when we pursue social policy is not easy. For instance, we stated that all individuals should be able to have food, shelter, clothing, education and medical care. How should we do it? Should we send an automatic payment to people at the start of each month as a kind of Universal Basic Income? Prout takes another approach, and looks at the problem from the perspective of its fourth principle which states:

4. There should be a proper adjustment amongst these physical, metaphysical, mundane, supramundane and spiritual utilizations.

While we want to make sure that no individual is deprived of his or her necessities, we also want people to develop all their capacities. If they receive a large automatic payment each month then they may not have any incentive to work or to acquire new skills or develop themselves. They will suffer, and society will be deprived of dynamism and innovation. In this situation, there will not be maximum utilization of our human resources.

An improvement on the concept of universal basic income is to guarantee employment at a living wage: employment that will provide each person with enough purchasing power to get the minimum necessities and as many amenities as are possible. Prout seeks to create a society that is prosperous and goes beyond providing bare-bones subsistence to its people. Today in the U.S. there are many people working two and even three jobs just to make ends meet.

One of the big challenges of providing employment in the years ahead will be automation. A progressive society could meet this challenge in a way that will help enhance human development. Under capitalism, automation allows corporations to produce more with less labor, and that is why new innovations often result in workers being laid off. In a society where the predominant business structure is cooperative, technological advances that boost productivity will have another result. The working time of all the members of the co-op will be reduced, and their income will remain the same or even increase.

Think about it. Science and technology have transformed this planet, and yet humans are still working 40-hour weeks, and in some cases much more than that just to get by. Some studies even show that hunter-gatherers have more leisure time than people working in agriculture or industry.[9] If we only had to work a few hours per day, then what would we do with ourselves? Maybe we could learn another language or cultivate our artistic skills, learn a musical instrument, travel, take part in sports, have time for meditation and other forms of self-development. All of these are activities which will result in greater human development and maximum utilization of our human resources.

Just as we must get the balance right between individual and collective needs, we also need to prioritize human skills and protect and enhance rare qualities. Intellectual and spiritual development are rare qualities when compared to physical ability and if someone is gifted intellectually or spiritually it is much better to educate and employ that person where his or her rare talent lies. Einstein probably could have swept the floors at Princeton University just as well as the janitors, but it would have been a loss to society if he did not go to work in the physics department of the university.

If we can balance individual well-being with collective well-being and build our society in a way that will bring out the best in as many people as possible, then we can count this as success. However, we cannot guarantee that policies that work well in the present will be appropriate in the future. That is why the fifth principle of Prout states:

5. The method of utilization should vary in accordance with changes in time, space and person and the method should be of a progressive nature.

No one can stop movement of the planet around the sun and the changes that come with the progression of time. What we call "cutting edge" today will be quaint and outdated in the future. In such cases, humanity can keep its basic principles intact, but the policies employed to carry out the principles must change in accordance with the needs of the time.

For example, when we think of utilization of physical resources today, we look to the issues of mineral extraction on earth and we debate about whether we should be extracting oil from shale using fracking. In the future we may be talking about mineral extraction on Mars!

Various technological innovations were sometimes resisted in the past because of fear of the unknown, but it is better to embrace the innovations because they will allow us to use our time for self-development. As we have already noted, each technological "advance" comes with corresponding challenges and unexpected side effects, but it is best to face these challenges bravely and move ahead. Thus, our "method of utilization" will be progressive.

The fifth principle of Prout is a safeguard which will allow Prout to keep its relevance far into the future.

Enacting and maintaining the economic structure, policies and principles of the Proutist model will also require important changes in government and leadership. The next sections address these issues.

Leadership and the
Social Cycle

Humanity can survive and flourish in the years ahead, but only if there is a group of intelligent, moral, wise and compassionate people who wish to participate in this task and take up the role of leadership. What makes a good leader? Can we do something to develop the best in people so that they can play a role in guiding society?

Before we tackle the demands of leadership head-on, an overview of history is helpful. Sarkar outlined a cycle of leadership patterns that spans the whole of human history and understanding this pattern of social change is extremely important today.

According to Sarkar, history moves in way that is determined by the leadership style of an era. At the birth of human society, in the Old Stone Age, humans were struggling for survival. Matter was predominant, and the minds of people were dominated by matter. This was the Age of Laborers.

Among the early humans there were people who had less fear of the dangers facing them, and who were physically strong as well as bold and with a martial spirit. These warriors emerged as the leaders and eventually this leadership of the bravest and strongest led to the institution of monarchy. The whole panorama of ancient history with the rise and fall of various empires is what Sarkar calls the Age of Warriors.

As the warrior-kings conquered territory and as the needs of society became more complex, another type of leadership emerged. The warriors needed help to produce their weapons of war and they also needed people who could administer the huge territories that were conquered. Intellectual capacity was every bit as important as physical brawn in this new era and this need was fulfilled by ministers and ecclesiastical figures who soon became the de facto leaders of society. Sarkar calls this the Age of the Intellectuals and though monarchy was the prevalent form of government the kings were crowned by the popes and religious leaders and it was the advisors and religious leaders who were the actual rulers during this era. Sarkar calls this form of government "ministocracy" and it was the prevailing system in the Middle Ages.

But just as the warriors gave way to intellectuality and religiously-inclined people, this new ruling class was eventually supplanted by people with a different skill set. The leaders of the Intellectual era had a hankering for the finer things of life. Spices, silk, jewels and other commodities intrigued them, and traders and merchants were dispatched to the Orient to procure them. Soon, a rising class of merchants and entrepreneurs emerged as the dominant force in a society that evolved into the Age of Acquisitors or capitalists. During the Middle Ages monarchy ended up as a de facto ministocracy but in the age of capitalism democracy became the preferred form of government. Our contemporary era is thus the age of capitalism with its twin sister liberal democracy. Although capitalism has been around for several hundred years this is not the "end of history." The wheel of history, the wheel of the Social Cycle is still in spin. What will come next?

To understand what comes next it is important to realize that the social cycle describes different psychological types that are dominant in each era. The fearless warriors who dominated the period that we know as ancient history believed that with their physical might they could overcome obstacles. In the Middle Ages, the approach of the intellectuals, ministers and ecclesiastical authorities was to dominate the world with their mental prowess. In the present capitalist era, leadership is vested in people with an acquisitive mentality, and they believe that they can use their intellect to acquire wealth and dominate the social and political systems. The psychological types of the leaders gave the color and flavor to each era; however, in every time period there existed warriors, intellectuals and merchants, living side by side, along with the workers. In fact, in a single family you will find individuals who embody these different traits. Thus, for Sarkar, the classes in a society, whether they be workers, warriors, intellectuals or acquisitors (capitalists) reflect psychological differences among humans and not income levels, or other commonly understood indications of class.

According to Karl Marx, the end of the capitalist era would be characterized by extreme concentration of the means of production in the hands of a few capitalists, and finally the exploited mass would revolt and overthrow capitalism. Marx saw two classes in conflict, the capitalists and the workers. Sarkar, however, took a more nuanced view.

In his book *Human Society*, Sarkar observed that in the capitalist era, intellectuals and warriors are reduced to the condition of struggling workers, worrying about how they can make ends meet. Like Marx, Sarkar believed that the excesses of capitalism would culminate in revolution. However, he observed that this revolution would not be led by rank and file workers, but by intellectual-minded or warrior-minded people. Recent history proves this to be correct. Lenin, for example, was not a laborer!

In every age the dominant social class first governs, introduces some innovations and then starts to exploit. There is good and bad in every era. When the warriors took over, they provided protection and security and humanity and began building advanced civilizations. However, as monarchies were established, warriors exploited society and engaged in useless combat.

Similarly, intellectuals broadened society with more learning but later exploited the same society through religious dogma and finally through religious wars. Capitalists brought in the commercial and industrial revolutions and added enormous wealth to society but ended up oppressing all the other classes of society.

Movement from the age of workers through the age of capitalists ending in worker revolution is one full rotation of the social cycle. One would expect that at the end of the capitalist era, workers would lead a revolution and establish a new system, and slogans such as "dictatorship of the proletariat" proclaim this idea. However, at the end of the capitalist era there is no worker age or worker society. After a period of revolution, disruption and anarchy, power quickly passes to the warriors (something that did occur in Russia, China and Cuba) and then a second age of warriors emerges. After the warriors come the intellectuals and then acquisitors. And, according to Sarkar, this cycle will go on and on.

History can be pictured as a roller coaster. There is an ascending phase when a new era is beginning and innovations and progress take place, then there is a peak point and after that a decline which can become a steep plunge, during which exploitation occurs. At the bottom of the trough there comes another upward surge which represents the new social class starting their upward journey and so on.

Sarkar noted that there is a way for humanity to avoid the steep declines that come when the prevailing social class starts to exploit society. He said that leaders who embodied the best qualities of all the classes and were imbued with morality and honesty could emerge. These spiritual revolutionaries Sarkar called Sadvipras. Sarkar explained that Sadvipras would be declassed individuals who would not favor any single class and that they would station themselves at the nucleus of society. They would carefully watch society and when there was a sign of exploitation, they would initiate change and bring in the next era.

Sarkar elaborated on the role of Sadvipras:

"Those spiritual revolutionaries who work to achieve... progressive changes for human elevation on a well-thought, pre-planned basis, whether in the physical, metaphysical or spiritual sphere, by adhering to the principles of morality, are Sadvipras... the duty of the Sadvipra is to see that the dominating class does not take recourse to exploitation. The four classes – the toiling class, the warrior class, the intellectual class, and the capitalist class – have remained well defined in the cycle of human civilization, and the gradual domination and decline of each class shall continue to occur in this cycle.... The function of a Sadvipra shall, therefore, be to see that the dominating or the ruling classes do not have any scope for exploitation."[10]

There will always be changes in society and there will always be the possibility that one class will try to exploit the others, but if humanity can bring forth leaders who can best be described as spiritual revolutionaries, then exploitation can be nipped in the bud, and the roller coaster of history can be smoothed out.

So, in summary, we require leaders who are moral and honest, and who look out for the well-being of all of humanity and not any single segment of it. We need leaders who are true public servants and not trying to line their own pockets or favor their own community. Can we find such people? In times of crisis and struggle, history shows that exemplary individuals do emerge in the form of freedom fighters, revolutionaries, social leaders and saints, and they certainly will come forth now and, in the future, as well.

What are universal principles of morality?

The first and foremost quality of the exemplary leaders is that they are grounded in morality. So that is why it is important to define what we mean by morality. We really need to define it because there are so many standards of morality based on different social and religious codes of conduct and if we want to build common institutions for all of humanity, we need one standard that applies to all. Sarkar looked to the ancient moral pillars of the yogic tradition, Yama and Niyama, as a base, but gave them a modern interpretation making them fit for a wide application.

There are ten principles.

The first five help people to live in harmony with the society around them. In Sanskrit they are known as Yama.

1. Not intentionally injuring others by thought, word or deed. The Sanskrit term for this principle is **Ahimsa.** In our daily individual life, we should not do actions or say things which will hurt others, but we can defend ourselves in self-defense if we are attacked. In India this principle was sometimes taken to an extreme by people who didn't till the soil, lest worms be killed in the process. Sarkar's interpretation of ahimsa allows for humans to live in the world and do what is necessary to maintain life, but to exercise restraint to prevent unnecessary harm to humans and other living beings.

2. To think and to speak in the spirit of welfare. This means benevolent truthfulness; that is, we should speak truth to others. However, if the uttering of exact truth will not be helpful to someone's well-being, then we should refrain from saying those words or say something else. The classic case is what you should do if someone comes to your house and asks, "Where is Joe, I want to beat him up," and Joe is in your living room. If you speak the exact truth, then your friend will be harmed. If you say, "I haven't seen him this evening," it will not be a fact, but it will be in the spirit of welfare. The Sanskrit term for benevolent truthfulness is **Satya.** Looking out for the welfare and well-being of others is one of the pillars of morality.

3. Non-stealing. We shouldn't take what doesn't belong to us. All codes of ethical conduct include this precept. Stealing is often direct, when someone takes a physical good that is not theirs, but it can occur in other ways. If someone plans to steal something, but refrains because he or she sees someone watching then it is a type of mental theft. If someone deprives others of a payment which they should have received, it is indirect theft. When someone sneaks into a theater or event, he or she has not taken any physical object, but has deprived someone of something they should have received. The principle of non-stealing is called **Asteya** in Sanskrit.

4. Treating all beings and things as an expression of Cosmic Consciousness. Prout is based on the idea that all living beings and the inanimate world are inseparably linked together. We are all in this together, and we must treat everyone as part of our large extended family. Instead of seeing another person as a "thing" to exploit, we should treat him or her with the utmost respect. This concept in Sanskrit is known as **Brahmacharya.** Seeing and treating all people and all living beings as expressions of the same consciousness.

5. Non-accumulation of things which are super-fluous to our actual needs. We all have basic physical needs and must strive to fulfill them by acquiring various goods. However, when we accumulate more than what we need, it is detrimental to our own well-being and can have a detrimental effect on society. The inordinate wealth accumulation of a few individuals often results in the inability of others to meet their basic needs. This principle applies not only to individuals but also to nation-states. It is called **Aparigraha** in Sanskrit.

Niyama

This is the second set of moral principles. Niyama is a Sanskrit word describing regulated conduct in relation to our self-development. The previously stated principles of Yama help an individual reach harmony with those around him or her. The next five explain how we can achieve inner harmony.

1. Maintaining external cleanliness and purity of mind. Keeping our body and environment neat and clean has an uplifting effect on our mind. Cleanliness is also an internal matter, and if we select our food carefully it will help us achieve a balanced mind. This principle also has a mental component. Just as we avoid stepping in mud and dirt to keep physically clean, we should also avoid things in the environment which bring us down mentally. Pornography is a case in point. The practice of maintaining physical and psychic cleanliness is termed **Shaocha** in Sanskrit.

2. Contentment of mind. It is not how much you have that counts, but how content you are with what you have, according to this principle of yoga (**Santosha** in Sanskrit). A humble laborer who is satisfied with his or her takings of the day is richer than a millionaire who remains unsatisfied. If someone accumulates too many material things, it is usually impossible for that person to attain mental contentment. Thus, principle five in the Yama - non-accumulation of unnecessary things - is tied to the attainment of contentment of mind.

3. Selfless service. Helping to alleviate the sufferings of others, even at the cost of our own comfort, is an important step to achieving inner peace and perfection. Service is not business. Whatever is done in the name of service should not be attached to remuneration either in payment or publicity. In the yogic tradition this concept is called **Tapah.**

4. Self-study. We should read, truly understand and imbibe the spirit of inspiring literature and other books of learning. This concept is called **Svadhyaya** in Sanskrit.

5. Moving toward ultimate self-knowledge through contemplation. Meditation on the consciousness at the core of our being is known as **Iishvara Pranidhana** in yoga. This practice enables a person to answer fundamental questions about his or her purpose in life and to find inner peace.

Can We Govern
Ourselves Properly?

"All animals are equal, but some animals
are more equal than others."
— George Orwell, *Animal Farm*

T HE ECONOMIC IDEAS OF PROUT which I
have outlined here may appear to be rational
and fair but bringing them into a concrete reality
will be a true challenge. The experiments in implementing various kinds of socialist models during
the 20th Century ended with dysfunctional, tyran-
nical states as satirized by George Orwell in his
book *Animal Farm*.

An important part of the effort to build a fair
society is the structure and functioning of the government. So far, the best form of government that
humanity has come up with is democracy, which
literarily means "rule of the people." However,
democracy as it is currently practiced often ends

up becoming plutocracy, the rule of the rich, or in its worst cases kleptocracy, the rule of thieves and finally, foolocracy.

Democracy could stand for some improvements, so let's consider some proposals from Prout's founder, P.R. Sarkar.

Eliminate political parties. Political parties emerged in 17th Century England and took time to become completely established. Today it may be hard to imagine a democratic system without political parties. But, do we really need the parties? A system in which candidates must stand on their own merits and their own personal record of service would be preferable to one in which a candidate hides behind the screen of a political party. If we required each candidate to publish his or her program in black and white, and then held them accountable to that program (by allowing for recalls in case they did not carry them out) it would provide transparency and accountability. We wouldn't need to know about their membership in a political party.

Political parties are not the only obstacle to an improved democracy. The quality of the electorate needs to be upgraded. There are four important conditions that must be met if a democracy is to function properly.

1. Minimum Economic Requirements must be guaranteed: Where there is exploitation and poverty, democracy cannot work properly. Deprived populations can easily be fooled by unscrupulous politicians.

2. Education: If the voters are illiterate then they can easily be misled by dishonest candidates. In some countries, elections are bought by politicians who supply blankets and other goods to downtrodden and illiterate segments of the country. Education needs to be free of charge and untainted by partisan interests. If the electorate is educated, then it will be more difficult for candidates and politicians to whip up hatred and narrow sentiments that could lead to disaster.

3. Social, economic and political consciousness: Even educated people can be fooled if they do not have deep knowledge of the major issues of the day. Many elections are fought based on slogans such as "lower taxes," "fiscal responsibility," "stop inflation," etc., but most people do not have a clue as to what these words really mean. In the recent past, millions of people were killed in wars in which the forces of fascism, religious hatred, and nationalism were unleashed, yet many people do not have the historical knowledge that would alert them to these dangers in the present day. Once again it is the duty of the educational system to help bring about the social, political and economic consciousness that could make the electorate capable of making the proper choices.

4. Morality: A recent, and disgraced, former U.S. president famously said, "I am not a crook." However, if 51% of voters do not maintain a high standard of morality, then crooks will be elected to office again and again. Raising the standard of morality in an entire country or of a society is not an easy matter, but we do not have a choice. If we want a functioning democracy, we will need to raise the moral standard of the younger generation, through schooling, mass media and the personal examples of our public servants, so that they will be able to make the proper choices when they cast their votes.

Global Governance

A GAINST THE BACKDROP OF the universe, the earth is a small planet and human beings must learn how to live together in harmony on this small planet. The best way to minimize the possibilities of war and to safeguard the rights of all people is to establish a global government. In addition, humanity now has to deal with environmental and health issues which transcend the jurisdiction of individual nations. Previous attempts in the 20th century in this direction, namely the League of Nations and the United Nations, have not been adequate and it is time to move to a better level of global coordination.

In his book, *Problems of the Day*, P.R. Sarkar laid out a concept of world government that could be achievable soon. He advocated the establishment of a bi-chambered world government. One chamber, the lower house, would have representation based on population and the other chamber, the upper house, would provide equal representation for all nations. The upper house would not be able to pass a law unless it has first been passed by the lower chamber, but the upper house in which all countries are represented would also have the right to reject bills passed by the lower chamber.

Sarkar envisioned a stage-wise movement toward world government. In the first phase, the world body would only be able to frame laws and administration would be in the hands of governments of the individual countries. In a later stage, the world government would also have administrative authority and a world militia at its disposal. In the past, world government was considered a utopian dream, but soon, it will become a necessity.

Building a Universal Society

THE WHOLE IDEA OF Prout is to build an economic and social system that will suit a united humanity living together as a harmonious family. When Sarkar first started talking about this in the late 1950s and early 1960s, he used the term universalism to describe this worldview. Instead of identifying with a nation-state, race or religion, it would be far better for people to look upon themselves and every human being as a member of the same human family.

This is, of course, easier said than done. In 1982 Sarkar wrote *Neohumanism: Liberation of the Intellect* and in that book, he deftly identified the problems which prevent us from looking upon our fellow humans as brothers and sisters. He noted that people usually first identify themselves with their geographic area or a particular social group rather than humanity in its entirety. In addition, he said that even when people start to think of lofty concepts like human rights or international fraternity, they sometimes neglect the needs of other living beings. He proposed a spiritually-based, ecologically grounded humanism, which he termed "Neohumanism," as the solution to the narrow viewpoints which prevent the attainment of love for all of humanity and other living beings. He elaborated on how humanity could go beyond narrow sentiments through education, developing a questioning and rational mentality and through spiritual practices. He also gave importance to the existential rights of all living beings and expanded the arena of human rights to include plants and animals. Neohumanism is thus the social and ecological outlook upon which Prout rests.

In his earliest writings on Prout, Sarkar also identified four common factors that will be needed in order to build a universal society.

1. Guaranteed availability of the minimum necessities of life. If large segments of the human society are unable to procure even the necessities of life, we will never know peace and harmony. We must make sure that every individual has access to food, clothing, education and medical care, and, as we outlined above, Prout's method for supplying these necessities is through guaranteeing employment that provides adequate purchasing power or, stated another way, employment at a living wage.

2. A Common Philosophy of Life. In the past, humanity went to war over differences caused by conflicting religious beliefs and due to identification with race, nation and other relatively narrow points of view. If all of us will accept the idea that humanity is one and indivisible and that our goal is to achieve physical, mental and spiritual fulfillment, then this common vision will keep us united for years to come.

3. Universality in constitutional structure. As humanity learns to live together, we will need to cement this unity with the establishment of a world government. What seemed impossible yesterday is increasingly becoming a necessity today, and as stated above, Prout proposes a two-chambered world body that will eventually be able to safeguard the rights of all people and to reduce and eliminate the scourge of war.

4. A common penal code. Today there are significant differences from country to country over what is considered a crime and what should be the method of rectification for individuals who violate the laws of society. Based on the common constitutional structure and using the broad concept that "all those actions which help in the growth of the spiritual, mental and physical aspects of human beings in general should come under the category of virtuous deeds, and those actions which go against humanity in its spiritual, mental and physical development must come under vice,"[II] a common penal code should be crafted.

Conclusion:

When the Progressive Utilization Theory was first presented in the late 1950s, it was certainly viewed as a revolutionary or utopian vision. However, current events, specifically climate change, pandemics and the possibility of a global economic collapse, have caught up with the ideas of Prout and now the time is right for a fresh look at this theory and for its implementation as soon as possible. What I have written here is a brief guide to the salient parts of Prout and a glimpse at how it might be materialized. I encourage you to read some of the original works on which this booklet is based and to visit the websites offered by activists who are working to create an economic and social order that will give people of the world a chance to live in dignity and to fulfill themselves in all spheres of life.

Websites for more information

www.proutalliance.org managed from the U.S.
www.prout.info a global website based in Denmark.

Annotated Bibliography

Books by P.R. Sarkar

Problems of the Day (Ananda Marga Publications, Kolkata, English edition, 1959). This book was transcribed from a discourse given by P.R. Sarkar in January, 1958. It is a small but powerful booklet that presents ideas such as cosmic inheritance, decentralized economic development, spiritual revolutionaries (Sadvipras) and more.

Discourses on Prout (Ananda Marga Publications, Kolkata, English edition, 1993). This booklet is described as a "summary of lectures delivered by P.R. Sarkar to the First Conference of Proutists, October 17-22, 1959." It is a revolutionary book which emphasizes the need for a three-tiered economy and Sadvipra leadership.

Human Society (Ananda Marga Publications, Kolkata, 1987). This book was originally published in two parts in 1959 and 1963 and is now available in a single volume. Part 1 gives Sarkar's idea on social justice, education, justice and the various occupations, and provides the vision needed to build a society in the true sense of the word. Part 2 is an in-depth look at the Social Cycle and how the revolving dominance of leadership styles through the ages have impacted society.

Idea and Ideology (Ananda Marga Publications, Kolkata, 1959). Although this is primarily a book of spiritual philosophy, the last two chapters explain the place of the Sadvipras in the social cycle and the concept of cosmic brotherhood.

The Liberation of Intellect: Neohumanism (Ananda Marga Publications, Kolkata, 1982). Sarkar unfolds a spiritually-based and ecologically conscious reformulation of humanism, showing how divisive sentiments can be overcome.

Proutist Economics: Discourses on Economic Liberation (Ananda Marga Publications, Kolkata, 1992). This is a comprehensive compilation of Sarkar's essays dealing with the principles of Prout and their application. Topics addressed in this book include balanced economy, economic democracy, decentralization, cooperatives and agrarian revolution.

An Outline of Prout (Ananda Marga Publications, Kolkata, 2018). This is a topic-wise compilation of Sarkar's views on the social cycle, progressive socialism, economic democracy, economic dynamics and leadership.

Books by other authors

Principles for a Balanced Economy: An Introduction to the Progressive Utilization Theory by Roar Bjonnes (Prout Research Institute, 2012). Prout is introduced through a detailed look at its five fundamental principles.

Growing a New Economy: Beyond Crisis Capitalism and Environmental Destruction by Roar Bjonnes and Caroline Hargreaves. (Inner World Publications, 2018). The authors address current ecological and economic crises, advocating a new economic approach which goes beyond both left and right ideologies and pays attention to humanity's urgent need to distribute financial resources more equitably and environmental resources more sustainably.

After Capitalism: Economic Democracy in Action by Dada Maheshvarananda (Inner World Publications, San German, Puerto Rico, 2012). This is a thorough 350-page introduction to Prout's vision of a socio-economic system which can replace capitalism and achieve the good and happiness of all.

Tools to Change the World by Dada Maheshvarananda and Mirra Price (Proutist

Universal, 2019). This is a study manual based on Prout offering a compelling vision of a more equitable, sustainable, and just society that will empower people and communities.

Acknowledgements

I am deeply indebted to my late and great teacher, Prabhat Ranjan Sarkar, who introduced the Progressive Utilization Theory (Prout) in 1959. Without his inspiration, foresight and guidance, I could never have written this booklet.

I would also like to thank my friends and colleagues who read my first draft and gave me valuable suggestions for its improvement. Included here are Sohail Inayatullah, Alex Jackimovitz, Howard Nemon, Amal Jacobson, Dada Gunamuktananda, Mark Mayatiita Friedman, Tapan Mallik and Gustavo Monje.

Proofreading and editing was done by Andy Douglas.

Finally, I would like to thank Donald Devashish Acosta, the founder of Inner World Publications, for his supervisory editing, layout and publishing work. His guidance and encouragement were crucial to the creation and development of this work

Endnotes

1   Wikipedia, https://en.wikipedia.org/wiki/Commons

2   P.R. Sarkar, *Proutist Economics*

3   www.community-wealth.org

4   P.R. Sarkar, *Discourses on Prout*

5   (from the essay Economic Decentralization, in *Proutist Economics*)

6   P.R. Sarkar, *Problems of the Day*

7   http://www.latimes.com/business/hiltzik/la-fi-hiltzik-ceo-pay-20180220-story.html

8   *Ananda Sutram*, Chapter 5

9   Sahlins, M. (1968). "Notes on the Original Affluent Society", Man the Hunter. R.B. Lee and I. DeVore (New York: Aldine Publishing Company) pp. 85-89. ISBN 020233032X

10   The Place of the Sadvipra in the Samaja Cakra, *Idea and Ideology*

11   The Cosmic Brotherhood, *Idea and Ideology*